This book belongs to

……………………

RIDHZWORLD
PUBLISHING

Awakening Parenthood Volume 1

Author

Rommal Surana

RIDHZWORLD
PUBLISHING

First Printing Edition @ 2024
ISBN: 978-81-964238-5-8

About The Author

Rommal Surana

Rommal, a dedicated and compassionate counselor and remedial educator, boasts a proven track record in fostering holistic development. With an MBA in Finance and Marketing and specialized training in Child and Adolescent Counseling, she brings a unique blend of financial acumen and psychological insight to her role. Rommal's deep commitment extends to assisting home-schoolers and children with learning disabilities on a personal level. As the Founder and CEO of the Nanhagyan Foundation, she actively contributes to the mental and emotional well-being of individuals.

Her accolades include prestigious awards such as the Bhartiya Shiksha Padma Bhushan Puraskar and the Dr. ABJ Abdul Kalam Shiksha Sarvoch Samman. Co-author of four books and a certified practitioner in various therapeutic techniques, Rommal leverages her expertise to create a positive impact on the lives of those she serves.

Preface

Welcome to the enriching world of parenting through short stories. In the labyrinth of life's challenges, there exists no greater odyssey than that of raising a child. Parenthood, with its myriad twists and turns, demands an unwavering commitment, boundless patience, and a reservoir of love that knows no bounds.

In the tapestry of our everyday lives, parents encounter a kaleidoscope of trials and triumphs, joys and sorrows. From the early morning rush to the bedtime tuck-ins, each moment is a testament to the profound journey of nurturing and guiding the next generation.

This book embarks on a remarkable voyage, weaving together tales that mirror the struggles and victories inherent in the noble art of parenting. Through the lens of storytelling, it illuminates the universal truths that resonate within every household: the delicate dance of discipline and compassion, the balancing act of setting boundaries while fostering creativity, and the constant quest for harmony amidst the cacophony of daily life.

Here, amidst these pages, you will find echoes of your own experiences—the laughter that fills the air during playful moments, the tears shed in times of uncertainty, and the quiet strength that binds families together through life's storms.

What sets this collection apart is its unwavering dedication to offering diverse perspectives and innovative solutions. Through the lens of storytelling, it invites us to explore new avenues of understanding, to embrace the power of empathy, and to celebrate the beauty of resilience in the face of adversity. As you immerse yourself in these tales, may you find solace in the shared journey of parenthood, draw inspiration from the triumphs of others, and uncover hidden gems of wisdom that illuminate the path forward. For within these stories lie the seeds of transformation, the catalysts for growth, and the keys to unlocking the boundless potential that lies within each of us.

In a world where the only constant is change, let us embark on this adventure together, guided by the timeless wisdom of storytelling and the enduring power of love. For in the tapestry of parenting, every thread—no matter how small—contributes to the vibrant mosaic of family, resilience, and hope.

So, dear reader, I invite you to embark on this journey—a journey of discovery, of reflection, and of renewal. For within these pages lies the heart and soul of parenthood—a testament to the enduring power of love, the boundless potential of the human spirit, and the transformative magic of storytelling.

With heartfelt wishes for a journey filled with joy, growth, and endless possibilities.

Warmest regards,

Ram Verma
TEDx Speaker, NLP Wellness and Parenting Coach

Table of Content

Table of Content

Table of Content

1

Belief - Can Make Or Break!

Before anything in this world is created in the physical plane, it is first created in the mental plane" - Law of Creation. To elaborate on the point, I am going to share this experiment conducted by some scientists.

A prisoner in France had been sentenced to death and a few scientists experimenting on the conscious and subconscious mind were permitted to put him to death through a scientific experiment.

The prisoner was made to lie down on a cot and the method by which he would die was explained to him, "We will gently remove all the blood from your body. When one bottle of blood has been removed, you will begin sweating. On removing the second bottle, your body will experience weakness. After the third, there will be darkness before your eyes. After the fourth, all your senses will stop working and unconsciousness will seep in. After a few hours of all blood being removed, you shall die."

After this, the blood was drawn out from the prisoner's body. After each bottle, he experienced

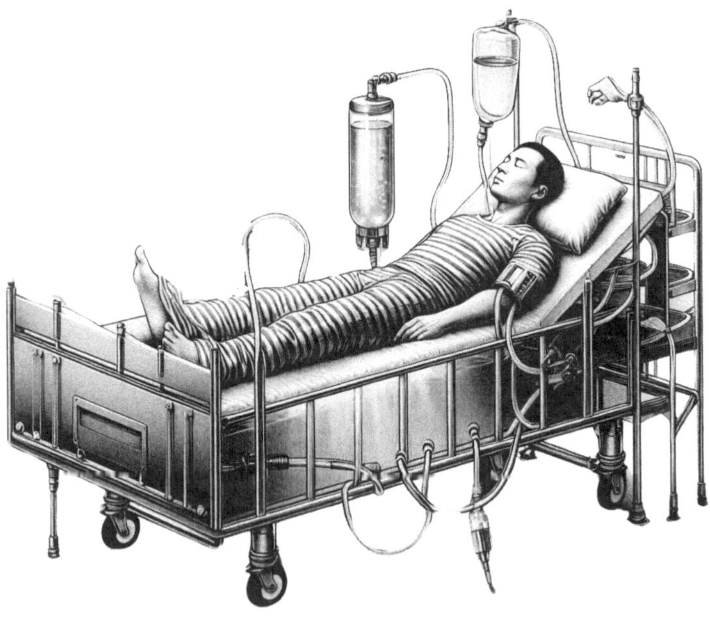

the exact symptoms that had been narrated to him and finally, he died.

However, just one bottle of blood was removed from the prisoner's body. The scientists had, in fact, arranged another tube below his bed that dropped water into the tube. The prisoner mistook this sound to be that of blood falling. He was constantly thinking, "All the blood is being drawn from my body and I am dying." This is the thought that was going on in his mind and it caused him to die.

When you think about something repeatedly, it seeps in and settles in the subconscious mind. This process is called programming the mind. We are continuously programming our mind right from our childhood. A child is unable to differentiate between what is right or what is wrong, but whenever he is given a thought, he imbibes it. This is how the mind gets programmed.

A mother tells her child, "Son, we are expecting some guests in our house this evening." Sure enough, the child sees the guests arrive in the evening. One day, she tells him, "It is going to rain today," and he experiences rain that day. Since the child is naive, he does not realize that his mother had called the guest over or that she had heard the news and had predicted the rain. The child feels whatever the mother says is RIGHT. One day she says, "You are good for nothing." He feels she is right and that thought goes deep in the mind and with time, it eventually settles or gets embedded there. In this manner, his mind is negatively programmed.

Let me share a live example of Chef Vikas Khanna. I was going through his interview with Anupam Kher, where he mentioned a few beliefs that his mother had given him. When he was born, his legs were inward due to which he would not be able to walk properly. This is what the doctor said. The surgery was performed within a few weeks. In childhood, he would wear those special heavy shoes made from wood. If someone would say, "Oh! Your child cannot walk properly." His mother would reply, "He is here to fly, not to walk." It was his mother's belief that led him to where he is today.

Every word said by us creates a belief in the child that would either make or break his life. Let us all be cautious and aware when using any negative or positive words or thoughts, especially in front of the kids.

Parenting Tips

- Be mindful of the language you use around your children, as their minds absorb and internalize what they hear.
- Instill confidence and positivity in your children by affirming their capabilities and encouraging them to believe in themselves.
- Encourage children to question and analyze information, helping them develop discernment and independence in their thoughts

2

What Do You Want To Become?

This beautiful story starts over a weekend when Vinay decided to wake up early. He opened his window and welcomed the fresh cool breeze which gently touched his face. It was peaceful and quiet with just the faint chirping of birds and the beautiful golden sky. He was completely mesmerized by the beauty and serenity of nature.

Navya, his daughter, was looking at her father. She pulled her father's clothes and asked what he was looking at. Vinay smiled and asked her to accompany him for a walk. Navya nodded. They wore their shoes and set off for a nature walk.

Vinay held his daughter's hand as they walked. After walking for a few minutes, they saw someone burning garbage on the roadside, a few steps further and there were polythene bags littered everywhere around. The sight was not pleasant at all. Navya said, "Papa, let's go from here and sit in a nearby garden." She said when she grows up, she will do something to keep the environment clean. Vinay encouraged her and explained to her that there was no need to grow old, she could do it even at her current age. With

a puzzled look on her face, she said, “I am too young, Papa.”

Vinay smiled and started mentioning names which Navya had never heard of. He asked if she had heard the names of Ishita Katyal, Tilak Mehta, Ridhima Pandey, Sreelakshmi Suresh, or Shravan and Sanjay Kumaran. Navya was confused and had no answer. Vinay told her that all of them were kids but very special ones and these were India’s entrepreneurs and change-makers. “All are from a different field but your age”, he added.

Ishita Katyal is the youngest Ted X speaker, aged eight, and author of the book “Simran’s Diary”. Tilak Mehta is the founder of “Papers N Parcels”, a startup dedicated to carrying small parcels and papers within Mumbai for an assured intra-day delivery. He is just 13 years old. Ridhima Pandey is an 11-year-old climate activist from Uttarakhand. Sreelakshmi Suresh is the youngest web designer and CEO in the world. At the mere age of ten, she had established e-Design – a venture which is now a web designing company. Shravan and Sanjay Kumaran are the youngest Mobile Application Developers in India. They are the brains behind Go Dimensions and are aged 15 and 17 years old, respectively.

"Age is an issue of mind over matter. If you do not mind, it does not matter." –Mark Twain.

All these kids saw challenges in the present. They wanted to contribute and make a difference in the lives of people. They did not wait for the future. They created the future.

Navya, how do you want to contribute to humans?

Many parents pose certain questions to their kids like - What do you want to do when you grow up? or What would you want to study? These questions are very often misleading. There is a more powerful question that we can ask our kids to empower them and prepare them for their future, "How do you want to contribute to the world?" These questions are directed towards making them ready for SOLVING PROBLEMS of the FUTURE.

When I asked this question to my six-year-old son, he expressed his interest in contributing towards clean air. I further asked him - how he planned to do that. He replied, “Perhaps I will create an Eco-friendly car, or I will invent a windmill that would convert polluted air to clean air.” More than his response, the path which parents show the kids for a better and brighter future is especially important.

Parenting Tips

As a parent, always ask your child what challenges they see around.

How can your child contribute to solve or find a solution to it?

It is easy to say to your child, "when you grow up what will you do?" Rather, guide them from childhood so they focus on their passion and not become a part of the rat race.

3

Passion Finds Its Way

"Allow passion to become your purpose and it will one day become your profession"
- Anonymous.

This quote reminds me of a girl whom I met in the month of Dec 2019, Sugandha. She is the daughter of a vegetable vendor and is physically challenged. Her body below her waist is paralyzed. The economic condition of her father deprived her of education after the 10th standard. I noticed that she had wonderful fine motor skills, and her hands could create perfect shapes.

Sometimes, there are some half-spoilt vegetables which are not usable for the customers. She would cut them as per the vegetable type, and her cutting techniques were commendable. She would do it as if she were using some mathematical tools to chop, dice, or shred the vegetable. In fact, her passion lay in cutting vegetables. I met her recently at a shop and could not recognize her initially. It was only when she greeted me that I recalled her. It had been about eight months since we last met, and there was a tremendous transformation in her appearance. I was curious and asked her about what she was doing. She said with high self-esteem, "I am an entrepreneur now. I have started a venture of supplying customized vegetable cutting to people." This was a little unfamiliar.

I asked her what exactly she was doing. She explained it in detail. She supplied chopped vegetables to various societies and hotels. She also had two staff employed under her who assisted her with this work. I was impressed with the vocabulary she has developed for different cutting styles. She mentioned a few techniques like Brunoise (Fine Dice), Chiffonade (Shredding), Julienne (Matchstick Cuts), Macedoine (Large Dice), and so on.

Sugandha said, "In this lockdown, maids were not allowed for household work. Chopping vegetables would take a lot of time. People were experimenting with new dishes and starting YouTube channels. This was an opportunity to make use of my passion. We started supplying chopped vegetables. There was good demand from our customers. We would take a customized order of vegetables to be chopped and supplied. As work progressed, I hired staff and interns from

the hotel management college. I have also started my online classes which have a huge response. With whatever I earn, I can upgrade my skills and help people." I was extremely impressed by her work and growth.

I have also started my online classes which have a huge response. With whatever I earn, I can upgrade my skills and help people." I was extremely impressed by her work and growth.

I took this case as a case study. I was reading the book Ikigai. The book is about "A reason for being" which talks about passion. In this case, Sugandha identified her passion and managed to identify market problems, where her passion could provide solutions. In the process, she also started making money out of it.

Your passion can fetch you money when you solve the market problem with that passion.

There are many examples of it. Kapil Sharma - Passion was humor, market problem - depression, sadness, stress, etc. The Kapil Sharma Show makes people stress-free. His show has been a hit, and he is able to make lots of money with this.

Parenting Tips

- **Identify your child's passion.**
- **Identify how your child's passion can solve market problems.**
- **Provide sustainable solutions for the ideas.**

4

Importance Of Pain

Once upon a time, humans decided to see Heaven. A few who were brave enough came forward and started praying. This prayer was powerful as it had devotion, affection, and dedication. This pleased God and He decided to fulfill the wishes of these brave people.

God said, "I am happy with your prayers. Tell me what you all want, and it shall be granted right away." "We want to see heaven," all said together. God said, "So be it." But there was one condition, "You all need to cross all oceans and mountains. Then, at last, you will find the gate of heaven. While doing so you need to carry these long wooden logs." These wooden logs were very heavy and long.

Such a scabrous journey with the burdensome log! All of them decided to start the journey and they started at their own pace. After reaching a certain milestone, one of them requested God, "May I cut a small portion of the log? It is bulky. I am unable to pull it." God replied, "So be it." He happily trimmed the small portion of the wooden log and restarted his journey.

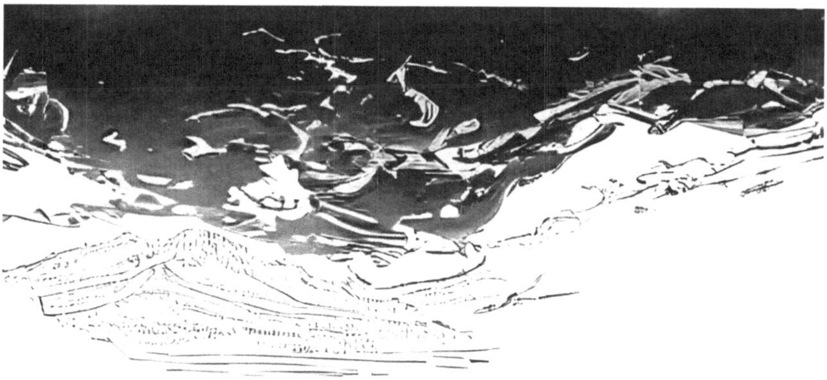

The speed of that man increased and upon looking at him, a few others also did the same. Of the entire team, there were just two left who were carrying the same log given by God. Sometime later, when everyone had crossed the ocean, that same man again asked God, “May I cut a small portion of the log? It is bulky. I cannot pull it further.” God replied, “So be it.” He again happily trimmed the small portion of the wooden log and began the remaining journey.

The speed of that man further increased and once again others followed him in trimming their respective logs. By now, almost half of the log was trimmed.

Finally, they could see the gate towards Heaven. However, as they came closer to the gate, all they could see was a huge valley. They realized then that they could only cross this valley by placing the huge log that God had originally given them. The only two men who had carried the wooden log as given were able to cross the valley and reach Heaven, while others could only be spectators.

Insights Gained:

1. Shortcuts can only give an edge but not the destination.
2. There is no shortcut to success.
3. Think twice about whom to copy.
4. Believe in God.
5. When one encounters any hardship, pain, or difficulties in life, it is important to understand that it has come because one has the caliber to handle it. No lock in the world, after all, is made without a key to unlock it.
6. One who embraces pain with faith and love is always rewarded. Kids, from an incredibly early age, need to be taught about how to face and tackle tricky situations rather than taking a flight or blame mode.

Parenting Tips

- Encourage children to view challenges as opportunities for growth and learning.

- Teach children the importance of persistence and determination in overcoming obstacles.

- Help children develop problem-solving skills by encouraging them to think critically and find solutions independently.

- Be a positive role model by demonstrating resilience in your own life and facing challenges with a positive attitude.

5

The Shift By Heels

Modelling or ramp walking is something which is always perceived to be a glamorous and high-confidence activity by most people who are unrelated to to the field. I had a similar peculiar stance towards this and could never associate myself with such an act since my childhood. One of the most probable reasons could be my low self-esteem, which was a companion since my early childhood. I had always carried and pictured myself as a tomboy, had a carefree attitude towards how I looked, how I walked, how I dressed up, and was far from even the basic world of makeup and lights.

As reality brings many surprises, recently, I did a ramp walk, not once but twice in a row, with different attire. Both the outfits were very unrelated to my personality and dress sense – a contemporary saree which I wore over leggings and the other was a black gown. This was with heavy makeup and hairstyling. The most striking aspect for me was the five-inch heel because until that day, the only heel I had worn was one inch. It was certainly a Herculean task to carry myself to such a height.

The First Shift

Something different started when I self-registered for this event. I had always been known as a counselor or parenting coach and here was a platform where I was recognized as an entrepreneur. Yes! I do have a firm, but for the first time, I identified myself as an entrepreneur who was adding value to society. The family and people who are close to us do not acknowledge the work done by us on an individual level - starting from something small and being self-employed.

The Second Shift

This happened when I first met the groomer. She was an elite personality with many international pageants in her crown. She started with an opening line, “You should know by whom you are being groomed”. This really penetrated my subconscious mind.

One should know how to value one’s own work. Your self-image should be reflected in your personality. Before anyone can perceive anything, you have already hit the bullseye. Others visualize you the way you want them to.

The Third Shift

I am a keen observer and I learn a lot from the environment around me. I was observing her the entire day and one thing that was very consistent with her was her confident and straight posture at all given points in time. Whether it was while taking a selfie with participants or guiding them for the walk; while doing her own makeup or dressing up for the event, her posture was consistently correct. This created the THIRD SHIFT in me. Whatever the profession, one cannot vanish in the professional environment. This comes only with deliberate practice and a lot of awareness. Skillful players like Virat Kohli and Jasprit Bumrah do not play a loose shot or ball even in net practice.

The Fourth Shift

My endeavor to register myself for this ramp walk was somewhere driven by my motive to evolve out of my comfort zone. I intentionally wanted to break the limiting belief that I had been carrying forever – my inability to carry myself well in heels. I had borrowed these five-inch high heels from a friend and wanted to ensure that I could walk comfortably and most importantly confidently wearing them. It was not an easy task to wear them and to be in them for over 5-6 hours was not easy. In fact, pain had engulfed my legs, especially my calf muscles were experiencing excruciating pain. It was time to be on the stage and I was able to manage the walk without any reflection of pain on my face.

At the end of the day, I was happy and satisfied and got my FOURTH SHIFT – the realization that one needs to make efforts to break the stereotype thoughts and ideas – created by self and the environment.

The Fifth Shift

I was accompanied by my 6-year-old son at the venue, and we were present there for almost 10 hours starting from 9:30 AM. His support needs special mention as even at this tender age, he managed to be there all by himself while I was busy with the dressing, styling, and makeup. The venue was safe, and a friend present there offered to check on my son frequently. Once the show was over, on the way back home, my son made a few statements that made me feel appreciated. He innocently asked, "Are you not proud of me? I cooperated with you the entire day, I made new friends, and we played a lot in the new place. I enjoyed your walk, and you were confident and loud even without a mic. You really rock, Mumma. I learned how to ask for help when you were not around. I am so proud of you. When are we going to experiment with a new similar venture?"

This made my FIFTH SHIFT, making me realize that kids are not an excuse but the reason to execute!

Parenting Tips

- Children tend to copy their parents. Be a role model for them.
- Explore a new avenue for yourself and make your children a part of it.
- Be ready to experiment with your new skills. This allows children to be flexible to adopt new things.
- Don't ask your kids to be independent. Create opportunities for them to be self-dependent.
- Don't use the excuse that the kids are young, and you cannot do this. Make them a reason and a part of the activity

6

What Creates An Impact : Feedback Or Fact

This story dates back to one fine day when an evening football class was taking place on the ground and all the parents were enjoying the tournament. I happened to overhear the conversation between two friends, sitting on the bench. I do realize that it is not good to intrude in private conversations with anybody, but I somehow could not resist myself.

It was not gossip but their perspective on looking at things differently. One of the friends, whose name happened to be Amrita, was complaining about what her mother-in-law said. Being a working woman, unfortunately it is common to receive comments like, “Are you giving enough time to your family? Are you aware of the changes happening for your son? What is the use of working if the family is suffering? Are you aware that with every step forward you are leaving a lot behind?” All of this and much more was being said by her mother-in-law, according to her.

In a common scenario, any friend would have consoled her and asked her to forget irrelevant things and move on. However, the other friend, Kalpana, had a new dimension to looking at things and her context in the complete scenario was unique. She only spoke a few sentences, but they were all logical and empowering.

She highlighted the fact that what her mother-in-law had said was simply her feedback and should not be taken as criticism. "Do not be too sensitive. She compares her parenting with yours, the amount of time she was available for her kids and the time you are available for your son.

Now let us validate the facts - Did you ask her what changes she is referring to? No. It is possible that she refers to the screen-time that your son demands. That has increased. If you look at the overall development of Parth, he is good. He is confident, friendly, academically excellent, well-mannered, hardworking, soft-spoken, and enterprising.", she added.

At times, people present their perspective as a fact. It is about you - whether to validate it or accept it as it is. We cannot always change the mindset of people; however, we can surely change our attitude towards the situation. Taking things personally can demotivate a person and make them feel guilty. Kalpana's words, somehow, got engraved in my mind.

Most often, women in our society – whether working or homemakers, face this situation of being advised by everyone around - resulting in degrading their morale and ruining their confidence levels. This happens to the extent that at times, the woman can start feeling guilty about the whole situation single-handedly. The best way is to peacefully verify whether the said thing is an opinion or a fact.

Parenting Tips

- It is essential to first validate anyone's thought as fact or opinion.
- As parents, we should teach our children to understand the depth of conversation as fact or feedback.
- Whenever required, teach them how to work on feedback and leave aside the opinion with strong belief.
- Develop critical thinking rather than a blaming attitude.

7

Quality Of Questions

There were two best friends, Seema and Dimple, who were living in the same residential society. Their kids attended the same school and were studying at the same standard. The kids were friendly with each other and often played together.

I was residing in their neighbourhood and had observed the way they brought out conversations with their kids. There was an enormous difference in the quality of the questions that were asked to the kids.

When the kids went to their preschool for the first time, they were overly excited. The mothers were eagerly waiting for them to come back from school and for them to share their experience. Seema asked her daughter if she liked the school. She was only expecting a yes or a no as an answer. Dimple, on the other hand, asked her daughter about what she liked in the school. This would help her understand the mental state of the child much better. The answer expected here will be much more than a simple yes or no.

When the kids were back from school, Seema

asked whether they had finished their tiffin or what was there for homework, etc. Dimple would ask a different question like “What did you enjoy in school today?” or “What did you learn today?”.

One fine day, both the kids returned home crying and seemed overwhelmed. They exclaimed their pain to their mothers, “You don’t love me?”. When Seema heard this, she began to give explanations of how much she loved her daughter. She reminded her of how she had bought clothes and toys for her, how she took her out every weekend, and tried to fulfill all her wishes. The daughter, however, continued to complain and felt that her mother did not love her. Dimple, on the other hand, asked a simple question, “What do you want me to do so that you know I love you?”. “Please hug me as soon as you come back from the office.” The emotional drama simply ended.

Now, it was the day when the first semester results were declared, but both the girls had performed poorly. Seema asked her daughter, “Why did you score less in the exams?” whereas Dimple asked her, “What needs to be done to score good marks in exams?”

Now was the time for the final semester examination results - Seema’s daughter still could not score well, but Dimple's daughter scored surprisingly well and topped her class.

Our brain is like a supercomputer. It always gives an answer, and the trick is that if you ask negative questions, the outcome is most likely to be negative; but if you ask a good positive question, you will get a positive result. For example, if you keep asking yourself why something unfavorable keeps happening to you - the answer you will receive is because you are incorrect somewhere. However, if you ask yourself for solutions about dealing with this situation, you will get a positive empowering answer. Plenty of times the brain asks a lot of questions, and most of these questions are negative, depending upon past experiences and upbringing most of the time.

As Tony Robbins quotes, "You can change the quality of your life by changing the quality of the questions you ask your mind."

Parenting Tips

Focus on asking open-ended questions to your kids. This makes them self-aware about their feelings and emotions. CLOSE-ENDED: Did you like living in Pune? OPEN-ENDED: What was it like to live in Pune?

Always ask empowering questions to kids. This enhances their emotional intelligence.

It's really important to ask questions that allow the child to think in depth about it.

Question level should be problem-solving, not hindering the personality of the child.

Content credit: Ram Verma

8

Right Words For The Desired RESULT!

There is a beautiful quote by Rumi which says,

"RAISE YOUR WORDS, NOT YOUR VOICE. It is the RAIN that grows flowers, not the THUNDER."

This reminds me of an incident when I was visiting a friend. We had not seen each other since college and today we were meeting after about nine years. She now has a six-year-old daughter. I was surprised to see her yelling at her daughter every five minutes for something or the other – for not keeping her things in the right place, for eating, for not playing properly, for not completing the homework. I watched the whole drama for two hours.

Once she was a little relaxed, I asked her the reason behind her anger. She strangely tried to justify her behaviour saying if she did not yell at her, she would not pay any heed to her in the future. This really amused me, and I then asked her if her daughter was even listening to her even after yelling. I also probed further and suggested what if she started talking politely to her daughter? She responded saying that she had tried everything in her soft, harsh, and polite approach but nothing seemed to work for her.

I tried to comfort her and reminded her of what she said when her daughter was watching television. She said, “do not watch TV”. When her daughter wanted to go out and play, she said, “do not go out to play.” When her daughter wanted ice cream, she said, “don’t eat ice cream”. To my surprise, she responded with a question stating what was wrong in her talking to her daughter that way. The conduct of many of us, as parents, is like this towards our children. I probed further and understood the reasons behind these statements. Why do they not give us the desired result?

What we use are words like eat, play, go - all of these are action words, and these acts can be visualized. Quite often, we subconsciously delete

the words NO or NOT from the statement. Hence when we say, “don't watch TV” or “don't eat ice cream” or "don't go out to play,” their subconscious neglects the No or Not. Now the statement transforms to “Do watch TV”, “do eat ice cream”, “do go out to play”. And that is what the child's really been doing.

We confuse the mind with incorrect statements and then blame the kids for not listening to us. What we wanted the kids to do above is to switch off the TV, stay at home, and avoid eating ice cream, then why not mention this directly. As parents, we need to learn the right ways of leading our kids. It can only be possible if practiced consistently and done constantly for at least a few weeks. We tend to just practice such corrective measures for a short span of time then declare them ineffective.

Parenting Tips

- The selection of the right words and pitch is particularly important to ensure that the kids listen to us.

- Avoid the usage of NO or NOT while giving instructions to the kids, unless it is important.

- To form a habit, we need to be consistent so that the kids also follow it.

9

Are We Ready For Change?

Some initiatives taken by schools these days are really thought-provoking and interesting. There has been a recent development in the school where my son goes. The school is now following an IE (Inclusive Education) system. This made me think and research about what Inclusive Education is. Inclusive Education (IE) is a novel approach towards educating children with disabilities and learning difficulties alongside those without, under the same roof. This is a beautiful initiative where all students are together in one classroom and community. Regardless of their strengths or weaknesses in any area, such an initiative seeks to maximize the potential of all students.

This initiative made me realize that children with and without special needs will study together. As a parent, I became doubtful, and many questions started coming to my mind. I knew that the school could solve my queries, but I decided to think and find solutions myself.

Is this initiative going to be beneficial for my child? Will the teachers be the same for everyone in the class? Will teachers pay more attention to kids with special needs only? What if our kids suffer? Should I continue with the same school or simply change it? All these questions kept wandering in my mind and gave me a thought that there would be other parents having similar thoughts.

There were a few parents who immediately withdrew their kids from the school. I was unsure and nervous. I recently watched a series called Good Doctor on an OTT platform for entertainment. In this series, Dr. Shaun is a surgeon with autism. He had excellent skills to diagnose symptoms in patients. He produces an innovative way to solve problems. Even the hospital management did not accept him easily despite him having potential like any other doctor. This helped me understand that Education is for all. We should not differentiate anyone based on differing abilities to acquire knowledge.

Every child has potential and is unique. The benefits which I see in Inclusive Education include:

1. This will help our kids to develop a sense of acceptance and belongingness with a difference.
2. This will enhance the emotional intelligence of our kids.
3. Our kids will also get opportunities to develop socially and academically.
4. Schools will come with best practices of instructions and the updated version of learning.
5. A step to develop a better society with more tolerance. As parents, we need to accept change, only then can our kids learn to embrace changes in life. We all believe that every child is unique and has a unique learning style. The time has now come to make beliefs a reality. So, are we ready for the change??

Parenting Tips

To have better emotional intelligence developed in our children, it is essential to live in an Inclusive Society.

School is a place where the child spends its quality time, if that is inclusive, our children will learn empathy, sharing, extending help, and caring concepts fast.

As we are living in micro families, tolerance and patience have decreased. Understanding the bond with children with special needs will develop those faculties in a child. Children who are buddies to special need children are observed with a better understanding of humans.

10

The Untold Story

International Women's Day is celebrated globally each year in the month of March. Women, from all occupations, are recognized for their work and contributions. Many award functions, talk shows, articles in newspapers, magazines, and interviews are organized to highlight the work that women are doing in all fields. Such events inspire women all over the world to share their extraordinary stories - stories of struggle, pain, hard work, handling abuse, and much more.

One of my friends once organized a beautiful session about self-defense for women on Women's Day. It was a great initiative under the name "Nirbhay Naari Abhiyaan". Many social workers, social entrepreneurs, schools, and individuals participated.

This reminded me of the NIRBHAYA case which has changed the mindset of society to a great extent. Moreover, a short film "DEVI" starring Bollywood actors was trending on the internet, which highlighted issues of sexual assault and rape. Many proactive measures to protect and safeguard women and children are being undertaken by both the Government and private institutions. The awareness about personal safety of individuals, self-defense techniques, and education about good touch and bad touch is being provided by the government, schools, colleges, and other institutions these days.

When we hear about molestation or rapes, the first thought in mind is to have the culprits behind bars. Once this is done, the story is over, or so we think, because another story starts here. The story of the Survivor - nobody asks about what happened to that survivor. Has the person rehabilitated in the world? Is that person fine, not just physically but emotionally and mentally? What happened to their family members?

All these questions are hardly ever looked upon or discussed. Working in child psychology, I come across many such related consultations. I once received a call from a woman who was concerned about her granddaughter and had observed some behavioural issues that needed to be addressed. I visited them and handled it the way I generally handle behavioural issues. Accordingly, I enlightened the mother and grandmother with what needed to be done. The child, aged 10 years, was gang-raped two years back. They shared this with me after she had left the room, and it left me shocked and speechless. My feelings at that point in time could not be expressed in words. Who did it? How did it happen? When did this happen? All sorts of questions engulfed my senses, but I soon realized that these questions could not change the situation which the child was undergoing.

The child was restless, frustrated, and had an eating disorder which she was unable to express. She was too young to even understand and comprehend what had happened to her. The whole family was suffering - her mother was suffering from depression, blood pressure, slip disc, and thyroid. She was weak - physically, mentally, and emotionally. She was encountering societal questions and glances each day, facing people who questioned her, blamed her, and even verbally abused her for the incident.

After this incident, people in society started blaming the family. No kid was allowed to play with the child. She was being communicated by these mean people about being impeached at the tender age of 8 years. The family relocated themselves to a new society where no one knew about this incident. The child was neither interested in going to school nor in doing any studies. The family had been through a tough time dealing with the police, doctors, and society. My mind kept questioning, what is the fault of this child? If she has no fault then, why can't she be treated as a normal child? Many will answer yes! She should be but when it comes to reality, these are the 'many' people who make living difficult for such victims and their families.

When working with this family, I reached out to a social worker. After having an interaction, the social worker appreciated my interest in helping the child and offered her help. She said, "You are doing an excellent job. I will assist in this case." Strangely, however, there was no response from her after the initial interaction that we had.

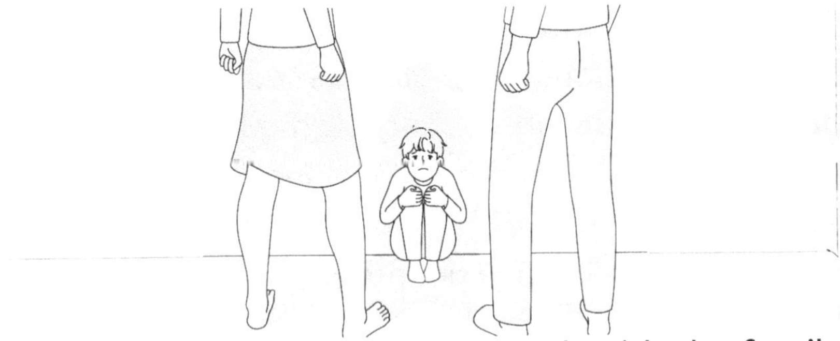

I am, however, continuing to work with the family to the best of my capacity to help. I feel even more responsible now, to help her live a normal and fulfilling life. While surfing the internet, I came across a few cases of child abuse which included those of Pranadhika Sinha Devburma (Founder Elan), Natasha Noel (Yoga guru, TEDx speaker).

In their speeches and talks, they mentioned a few things which were common:

1. They used to hate themselves.
2. They felt they were responsible for all the wrong happening in their life.
3. They believed that no one could love them.
4. They are a bad charm.
5. They used to self-harm by physically hurting themselves with sharp tools.
6. They felt that they do not belong in the normal world.

Most of the times, in articles we read or information that we come across, it is highlighted that it is essential to teach boys how to respect women. However, the fact that even boys are equally victims of child abuse cannot be negated. I want to request all my readers to extend help to

these survivors. If you get a chance, do meet them. Also, in such cases:

1. Please do not be sympathetic, rather be empathetic while treating them and offer the same respect and love as you would to any human.
2. If you cannot help them, at least listen to them and encourage them to take professional help.
3. Don't blame the family members, try to understand their condition.
4. Provide love, care, and faith that they are lovable and important to society.
5. Understand that growing in life is essential for them too.

Parenting Tips

As parents, it is important to teach children the importance of good touch and bad touch.

Parents should demonstrate a good role model to their child by treating everyone equally.

Visit orphanages, old age homes, blind schools, and other places like this. This may help the child to develop an empathic perspective towards unfortunate groups of people.

11

Healing The Childhood

The childhood of today is the manhood of tomorrow" - William Wordsworth

Our childhood is a significant part of our life and forms the base of our life. Our belief systems with regards to different relationships, self-esteem, fears, values, and the like are formed in this phase of life. Many are fortunate to have a happy and healthy childhood. However, there are a few who unfortunately go through physical and mental abuse causing trauma from this tender age. As a result, such children develop negative emotions resulting in low self-esteem, insecurity, loneliness, revenge, and such bothersome aspects of personality. Lack of love in childhood may also gradually develop into self-blame and self-criticism until adulthood. Thus, it is especially important to heal such childhood wounds, if any. Healing is essential for having a positive and contented adulthood.

Many personality disorders usually develop because of a toxic childhood like Narcissism, Sociopathy, and bipolar disorder in some cases. One needs to be aware of their symptoms, methods of identifying them, and then treating and healing them. It is possible to heal childhood scars on the mental and emotional level. There are tools and techniques available. Once you start working towards healing, please keep in mind that healing is a process and that unlearning and relearning do not proceed in a linear fashion; there are steps forward and steps back as you fall into old default patterns which might seem tackled. This is totally expected so do not judge yourself harshly and keep in mind that this is a marathon, not a sprint.

Ten signs of healing.

1. One gets better at naming one's feelings.
2. Even when things go wrong, one stops blaming oneself.
3. One does not sit and ruminate on old habits.
4. One can voice worries without hesitation.
5. One becomes resilient in handling rejection.
6. One becomes consciously aware of triggers.
7. One sets limits and respects them.
8. One becomes more aware of their capacity and capabilities for handling rough situations.
9. One begins to see oneself.
10. One can manage emotions with skills.

Parenting Tips

- Foster an atmosphere where your child feels safe expressing emotions without fear of judgment or punishment.

- Pay attention to your child's feelings and thoughts, validating their experiences and offering support.

- Establish predictable routines and boundaries to give your child a sense of stability and security.

- Encourage your child to build supportive relationships with peers, family members, and mentors.

12

How To Handle Sibling Rivalry?

The concept of joint families is prevalent in small towns in India. However, in metro cities, there are more nuclear families.

The term 'sibling' refers to children related to a family and staying together at one place. They can be maternal or paternal cousins or kids from the same parents. We hear a lot of complaints from parents about kids disagreeing with each other or fighting amongst themselves. Many times, they lack synergy among themselves. The word 'Sibling' denotes a lot of love and care for each other. The term "Sibling Rivalry" was coined to signify the differences that such kids seem to have among themselves. These differences can be projected through physical abuse, verbal abuse, or emotional gestures.

There are some key factors which result in sibling rivalry:

1. Chronological position in the family (elder and younger)
2. Age gap between the siblings
3. Gender

The beliefs and attitudes of parents play a vital role in the upbringing of children. Highlighted here are certain dos and don'ts for resolving such conflicts between siblings:

1. Do not make comparisons.
2. Do not dismiss or suppress your child's resentment or angry feelings.
3. Try to avoid situations that promote guilt in siblings.
4. Whenever possible, let siblings settle their own differences.

Some common mistakes parents make in managing Sibling Rivalry:

1. Taking sides
2. Ignoring appropriate behaviour

Simple Parenting Techniques That Work:

1. Whenever sibling rivalry progresses to excessive physical or verbal violence OR when the number of incidents of rivalry becomes excessive, act! - Talk to the kid about what is going wrong. Provide a proper solution for the problem, which might be either of these: - Ignoring the teasing. -Simply agreeing (in a kidding way) that whatever the teaser is saying is true. -Telling the teaser that enough is enough. -When these measures are not working, ask the person in charge (parent, babysitter) for help.
2. When the above does not work, introduce a family plan to help with the situation that provides negative and positive consequences for all concerned, such as: When there is any fighting or shouting, all involved will have a consequence such as a timeout or the temporary removal of screen time. -However, when we can go the entire day or afternoon or evening (whatever makes sense for your situation) without fighting, everyone will earn a privilege such as:

- (a) you can have a snack
- (b) I will read you a story
- (c) we will all play a game together

- (d) I will play outside with you (catch, etc.) or
- (e) you can stay up later. In short, reward them with situations where more parental attention and presence is provided.

3. A system for taking turns for trivial things:

- Who will sit in the front car seat?
- Who will push the button to the elevator? and so on.

Parenting Tips

- **Address excessive rivalry promptly by discussing the issue and providing solutions.**

- **Implement a family plan with both negative and positive consequences for behaviour.**

- **Introduce a turn-taking system for trivial matters to promote fairness and reduce conflict.**

13

Pieces Or Peace

Online spiritual practice sessions are usually overwhelming and not scientifically proven, and thus many gained from them. I once attended such a session, and this time I found the session very logical and practical. The trainer and the session moderator were talking about the different research conducted on Meditation. We all know meditation is good for physical and mental health. Practicing meditation increases our longevity and comes with many other benefits too.

In this session, the moderator talked about Meditation as a "Service to Humanity". This was something unique and different from all that I had heard until now. This made me curious, and I decided to research and understand this myself.

In the session, he talked about a research called the "Maharishi Effect". This meant that practicing the Transcendental Meditation® technique would produce measurable improvements in the quality of life for the entire population. This phenomenon was first discovered in 1974 and reported in a paper published in 1976. Here, the finding was that when 1% of a community practiced the

Transcendental Meditation (TM®) program, the crime rate was reduced by 16% on average.

This was interesting. If one thousand people meditate together for a certain period, positive changes like a remarkable decrease in crime rate, homicides, suicides, and road accidents were visibly possible.

While going through the research, a thought provoked within me: Within a family, we face stress, relationship turmoil, and many such limitations which disturb the state of mind of individuals and the environment of the family. Practicing meditation may improve this. Even if one person starts practicing meditation, the environment within each family is liable to improve. I started practicing a special meditation called twin heart meditation, to test this claim and was able to see the results with regular practice within only a few weeks.

I would thus urge everyone to experiment with any kind of meditation and experience the visible changes. It is by far the best way to serve humanity.

Reference Link

https://maharishi-programmes.globalgoodnews.com/maharishi-effect/research.html

Parenting Tips

- Pranayam and yoga rejuvenate the body. As parents, we should inculcate these habits in our lives and in our children's lives too.

- Meditation raises the vibration of the whole family. Inducing such a habit will strengthen the character of the child.

- Facing mental challenges, a competitive world, and financial challenges become easier, and productivity goes up.

14

Understand The Inner Child

I was recently a part of an educational summit, where many influential personalities were appreciated and recognized for making a difference in society, in their own way. I was also felicitated and acknowledged for my work.

To be honest, I suffered from many inferiority complexes during my childhood - be it looks, intelligence, or way of communication. I had never participated in any school event throughout my schooling years. I was an average student, not a bright one.

Being brought up in a joint family, I was constantly compared to my cousins. Throughout my formative and vulnerable years, I was constantly fed the thought, "You're good for nothing." This came to me from all directions, from family, peers, friend circles from school and tuition classes, whether directly or indirectly. The entire environment around me made my self-esteem, confidence, self-worth, and my self-image a big ZERO.

Not knowing how to deal with all this, I gradually became rebellious, sarcastic, closed, and unapproachable. My parents had never forced me to study harder or get better marks, yet I had an imaginary world where nobody ever understood me. I always dreaded coming back home. My pain was never visible, rather the aspects visible at the surface level in my personality were my frustration, anger, rudeness, roughness, and argumentative behaviour. I was singled out for those actions for so many years as everyone around me could only look at the surface level behaviour of mine.

I am sure parents of many teenage kids can relate to these traits in their children.

When I joined junior college, many things changed. In the unfamiliar environment, no one knew my past. The positive and encouraging atmosphere of that college really pushed my threshold to the next level. From an ordinary student, I rose to become Student of The Year! This boosted my confidence and changed my whole perspective towards my own life. The graph of my life shifted drastically from here.

Parents and teachers, please do not judge your kids by their behaviour or marks. Understand the root cause of behavioural outbursts. Many children do not understand why they behave in a certain manner. Even I had never understood it when I was at that stage and undergoing the situation.

It was the constant nurturing, love, and belief of my teachers and friends that released my suppressed emotions. It helped me regain my confidence, self-esteem, and self-worth. Help your children to vent out their suppressed thoughts and ideas. Give them time to gather their full potential before they are ready to take the leap!

Parenting Tips

- **Refrain from comparing your child to others, especially siblings or relatives.**

- **Create a safe space for your child to share their thoughts and feelings openly.**

- **Help your child identify their strengths and interests and encourage them to pursue them.**

15

Tell Me Something Interesting About You

Once at an event with about thirty participants, we were asked to introduce ourselves, covering six things:

• Name • Educational qualification • Region we belonged to • Hobbies • Something interesting about ourselves • Our scores

These seemed like quite simple things to answer. To my surprise, people were stuck when talking about their hobbies or sharing something interesting about themselves. Many of them were working in the IT sector or in a place where they spent more than 10 hours in front of the screen every day. This was the reason behind their hobby being listed as watching TV/web series or movies.
I was puzzled to know that even watching TV or movies could be listed as a hobby. Hobbies, as per my understanding, are something that we love to do at leisure.

Wikipedia says, "A hobby is considered to be a regular activity that is done for enjoyment, typically during one's leisure time, not professionally and not for pay."

Watching a screen, according to me, could not be a hobby. Even for "something interesting about

yourself" - many fumbled, while others just shared something for the sake of saying.

Truly, we do not know about ourselves. Today, at the click of a button, we get to know all kinds of information around the world. Have we forgotten to tap the button to our inner world?

The world is getting digital every second. Technology is upgrading every minute.

Let us not forget to rejuvenate our inner being with hobbies that connect us internally.

Help your children develop hobbies and encourage them to pursue them, because hobbies will be there with them when you are not around. Developing hobbies in kids will help them to phase out boredom, depression, competition, and connect them with who they really are.

Hobbies provide us happiness, bring out our creativity, and give us inner peace.

Parenting Tips

Encourage your child to explore different activities and interests to discover what brings them joy.

Show your child the importance of hobbies by engaging in activities that you enjoy and find fulfilling.

Provide opportunities for your child to express themselves creatively through arts, crafts, music, or writing.

Encourage balanced screen time and prioritize offline activities that promote physical and mental well-being.

16

Why?
'BUT'

In the Parts of Speech, the word 'But' is used as a conjunction. Everyone would know that it connects two statements.

Now, let us see how our subconscious mind uses the word 'But':

Here are two sentences. a) I will be successful, but I do not have resources. b) I do not have resources, but I will be successful.

Among Option A and Option B, which is a more powerful statement? Yes, Option B.

Isn't it interesting that the two statements - "I will be successful" and "I don't have resources" - have different meanings with the placement of 'but'?

Our mind negates the statement before 'But' and approves the statement after 'But'.

That is the reason the statement "I don't have resources, but I will be successful" is more powerful than "I will be successful, but I don't have resources."

To develop new beliefs and imprints, the subconscious mind lets us use 'But' wisely. Be aware of the placement of the word.

"My daughter is very obedient, but she is a slow writer". Use this instead - "My daughter is a slow writer, but she is very obedient."

Your mind will negate the first statement and will accept the next statement after 'But'.

We should be careful while speaking, especially with ourselves. Our subconscious mind works on our beliefs, the identity we create, the values we set, and the purpose we make. Negative self-talk is dangerous.

Examples:

- I prepare myself for exams, but I forget answers when I sit for exams.

- I want to lose weight, but I love eating vada-pav.

- Always remember, place the belief which you want your subconscious to accept and work more effectively after the 'But,' like –

1. I forget the answers during the exams, but I will prepare myself well.
2. I love eating vada-pav, but I want to lose weight.
3. Try using this in your daily life and see the change!

Content credit: Ram Verma

Parenting Tips

- Be mindful of the words you use, especially 'but', as it influences how beliefs are formed.

- Teach your child to use affirmations and positive language to build self-confidence.

- Lead by example by using constructive language and focusing on solutions rather than problems.

17

Who Needs My Time?

I was meeting my close friends after a long time. I was extremely excited. Manisha, Rama, Prerna, and I - we all had our own different lockdown stories to share.

Manisha had suffered from loneliness. She had learned how to utilize time in a constructive way towards the inward journey. Meditation, drawing, understanding her emotional state, and handling awareness had helped her a great deal.

Rama has a joint family. She was busy with household work all the time. Initially, she said she would be busy with daily chores. She never had time for herself. Looking after her old in-laws and a small baby, the world would end there. In this lockdown, she learned the art of time management, delegation of work, and teamwork. Now she was able to manage some time for herself while also maintaining a smooth flow and management of the household work.

Prerna had an interesting journey. Her husband is a software engineer, and her daughter is 8 years old. In this lockdown, Prerna started her professional journey. She is a certified yoga instructor and dietician. She expressed that her husband would be busy with work, meetings, sessions. Her daughter would be busy with online school and online activity classes. She would go cycling and play by herself. Both were busy. It was important for Prerna to know how to fill in the free time after finishing her work. This was a big challenge.

So, she started with online yoga classes and a YouTube channel for healthy recipes. She got busy with her class and video shoot and editing. She got a huge response and soon started with one more yoga batch. Editing a video took at least two to three hours a day. After finishing her household work, she actively engaged herself in these activities and was also being invited by various groups for collaborative LIVE sessions.

She was now being sought by her close relatives, who appreciated her for the excellent work that she was doing. However, there was one constant question from them, “Are you giving time to your family?”, “Nowadays you are busy”," Look at your daughter, she looks weak". These complaints would really disturb her.

When her mother said," Why do you need to do this? How much are you earning from this? Your husband is earning handsomely, then what is the need for earning? Pay attention to your family! You are always busy with this online stuff? It is ok to do something for engaging time but working for seven to eight hours is not acceptable. This is not a business that you are setting up." This really brought her spirits down.

How she had responded to her mother really moved me. She had said "Maa, Akaash (her husband) is busy with office work from 8:00 AM to 10:00 PM. After the office, he invests time in upgrading his skills or on Netflix. My daughter has online school and activity classes throughout the day. You kindly tell me, what should I do the entire day?" She further said," Maa, I do not do this for money but to keep myself engaged and utilize my time fruitfully. If in doing so, I can earn something, then where is the harm? Since I am doing this from home, even my daughter will be able to learn these skills from me. If instead I take a job somewhere, at least my eight to twelve hours will be completely occupied. Presently, however, if I am investing seven hours each day in my own venture, that too without much investment, is it not great? I am fulfilling all my responsibilities while simultaneously getting fame and respect. It is possible that I further expand my work and make it into a proper business model.

Many times, when a woman is doing a job, she is accepted and considered as a serious professional. When something is started from home, it is not taken as seriously. Family and close relatives are the ones who often hold them back. As a result, it is hard to find many women entrepreneurs working on a large scale. They are, many times, restricted to home tuition, beauty parlours, dance, music, hobby classes, cooking, sewing, embroidery, mehndi, stuffed toys, and such small-scale setups. There is a wider scope and spectrum beyond exploring things while we are at home.

I am exploring my horizon, what about you?

Parenting Tips

Emphasize the importance of adapting to new perspectives and ideas, promoting growth and understanding within the family unit.

Highlight the importance of recognizing good work, regardless of whether it's done at home or in an office.

Every family is equal and needs to fulfil its family duties.

Encourage family members to pursue their dreams and ambitions.

18

Mental Diarrhea

Chitra and Devina have always been the BFFs (Best Friends Forever) and were always seen together. They both studied in different schools and had distinct backgrounds, yet they were always together. They were both unique in their own way. Chitra was an outspoken and charismatic speaker, while Devina took time to open up. She was excellent with innovative ideas, execution, and connecting the dots. Kids of their age were amazed by her work. Devina and Chitra made a marvellous team.

However, for a few weeks, they were not seen together. I met Devina recently and could see her dimmed, confused, and lost in her own thoughts. Her spark, which used to be evident earlier, was missing. She had visited me but was incredibly quiet. She used to have a lot to share. I could easily sense that something was bothering her.

I knew her well, so I decided to ask directly, “What is the issue?”. She was not ready to respond. I then asked about Chitra, but the same silence. I further asked, “How is the preparation of the campaign going on?” She looked puzzled and anxious. It was now understood that something was wrong between the two friends.

I kept quiet for a while and gave her some time to think and respond. Devina started pouring out. “Aunty, I am frustrated, sad, angry, and disappointed with Chitra. I cannot explain the reason to her. Logically she assumes she is right, but ethically she is wrong. I do not understand why she copied all my ideas. Our concepts are usually different, yet she creates confusion everywhere. I am helpless.” She then stopped, took a pause, and restarted the conversation by highlighting some past incidents and random thoughts.

Honestly, I did not understand what exactly she was talking about or whatever she was referring to. Which concepts? Whatever she spoke was as if it was Greek and Latin to me. The only thing I understood was that she was suffering from MENTAL DIARRHEA.

I looked at her and said, “Devina, you are suffering from Mental Diarrhea.” She bewilderedly looked at me and said, “What??? I mean, what does it mean?"

I explained to her, “Our brain keeps on working right from our birth till our death, 24/7, even when our body rests during sleep. We are flooded with numerous thoughts, but most of these thoughts are useless, and this is what is known as Mental Diarrhea. You have no control over your thoughts, and you do not know how to properly comprehend or channel them. All you can think of are these negative thoughts and as a result, you have developed a state of mental diarrhea."

"Now the question arises, how to stop this. Think about this, Devina. Is there any copyright to the ideas that you have?"

"No, Aunty!" She spoke.

"Being ethical? Isn't it a subjective topic in this scenario?" "Yes, Aunty," she replied.

"Are you not collecting references from your past, only to justify the pain you are feeling today?" "Yes, Aunty," she replied.

"There are common people who are influencing the situation between you and her," "Hmm," she replied. "Is all of this stuff not disturbing you? Has this not diluted your efficiency to think and respond?" She strongly said, "Yes, definitely, Aunty.

I then calmly responded, "Accept the situation. Do not fight with it. You cannot control anyone, but the only one who can control you is yourself. Understand that what you give will come back to you in multifold. Today you are in a negative frame of mind, so you are attracting all negative incidents, thoughts, and people around you. See the same situation with a positive aspect."

"What positive aspect, my friend copying me? What positivity do I see in this?" she said in anger. "Don't you see an opportunity here?" I said. "See it this way, just because she is copying you, aren't you getting an opportunity to think differently? You have expanded your horizon and are thinking differently, new thoughts are coming to your mind, and more innovative things are on the way. Be honest and accept that it is just because of her that you are thinking in this manner. You should, in fact, thank her."

I added, "Devina, situations cannot change, but how you look at things can change. There is always a unique perspective to look at the same thing. Evaluate this, think about this." She was digesting this slowly and she got up with a smile and said, "Thank you for the help, Aunty, for giving me a new perspective to see this situation."

Insights Gained:

1. We all go through mental diarrhea. Let us try to be aware of what we are thinking.
2. Focus on conscious thinking.
3. Look at the same situation from a distinct perspective.

Parenting Tips

- **Help your child identify when their thoughts become overwhelming or negative.**

- **Teach your child to pause and reflect on their thoughts and emotions without judgment.**

- **Introduce mindfulness techniques such as deep breathing or meditation to help calm the mind.**

19

Paradigm Shift

I had always been part of a joint family, living together since birth. We were a family of thirty members and as a practice, women were meant for the kitchen and men for the office. This gender division had become a belief for me.

Ever since my childhood, there were a few beliefs which had been engraved deep in my mind. Things like men do not participate in household work, they were meant for the outer world while everything else had to be taken care of by the women.

As I grew up, the scenario saw a shift, women had started working. The change was happening but here a woman could work only while ensuring that her personal and professional fronts were responsibly managed and balanced together. She needed to set her equilibrium in all aspects of life. Then there happened the Lockdown!

Lockdown has significantly altered the old belief system and has, in fact, instilled new thinking patterns. With three consequent lockdowns, new thoughts have managed to make newer and stronger neural pathways and neurological connections, creating an altogether new belief system.

During this phase, I can see my husband and son extending their help and putting efforts towards daily chores like folding clothes, arranging utensils, or sweeping the floor. This has never happened before the lockdown. Once I had asked my son to help me with some household work and he had replied, “This is not my work, I have never seen Papa doing this. Why should I do it?”. At that time, I did not know how to explain this to my 6-year-old but today without explaining anything, things were happening in accordance because he was seeing his father helping his mother.

The point of concern here is not gender equality but the fact that “This is my house; every responsibility is shared. Whether it is cooking, sweeping, mopping, cleaning, dusting or anything else.” It is no longer a gender-based division of work, a more mature way of working and maintaining balance at home. When parents are working professionally and helping each other in household work, it sets a perfect example for kids and shapes parents as the right role model for the kids.

This lockdown has changed many perspectives

and classified ideas. Being a stay-at-home spouse or homemaker is not a shame or reason to feel inferior. It is, in fact, a matter of pride. The earlier questions about what a homemaker does at home have been practically cleared with this experience. This learning is here to stay and will not change in the future as this has resulted in a stronger bond between families and their members.

This lockdown has also brought another aspect of family into the picture. It has made people understand that the meaning of parent is “Mother and Father” not “mother or father”. In the Lockdown phase, families were spending their time together. The essence of the family, which was lost somewhere in daily schedules, meetings, deadlines was rebooting again in many families.

We once organized a Talent Hunt in our Facebook group. To my surprise, most boys were cooking, and girls were dancing. This made me realize that we are leading to a newer world, allowing individuals to choose what they want in life. Every parent is opening their mind to innovative ideas by allowing their kids to experiment with different fields, not just focus on academics.

Lockdown has silently changed many stubborn ideologies in a subtle and effective way.

Parenting Tips

- **Parents should actively participate in household chores to set a positive example for their children.**

- **Encourage children to see household tasks as shared responsibilities, regardless of gender.**

- **Discuss with children the importance of teamwork and cooperation in maintaining a balanced home life.**

Parent's Testimonials

It was really a very good experience for us as parents. After interacting with Romal mam, we got to know about many things that would help us to communicate with our child in a better way. I would recommend anyone who is worried about their child's behaviour to have a session with Romal mam, it would surely help.

- N Gupta

We had consulted with Romal mam for our son. We talked about various aspects of delayed milestones and how to mitigate them. She gave us several tips which seem simple and yet effective. After consulting with her, we came to know of new things which will surely help us to track the progress. Will definitely recommend to parents who want a fresh view as she is empathic as well as great listener to understand the pain points parent usually go through. As well as looking forward to the tips and various help material shared by foundation.

-Amit Srivastava

I went for my daughter to Mrs. Surana and came back with solutions. She is very positive and leads by example. She gives practical solutions and they prove very effective and make absolute sense. Just in a day, I can see positive changes by applying her techniques which has given me clarity and lots of peace. I would recommend her to every parent who has been feeling lost and having no clue how to deal with parenting problems.

- Neha Yagnik

We have seen the efforts of our child however were not sure, what we can do to minimize the efforts for her to overcome the challenges that she faces in the competitive world. As a concerned parent, we approached Romal ma'am for help. She not only helped us understand our child better but also gave inputs to focus on the pattern rather than the challenges

- Seema Sharma

Me and my wife with our son visited Mrs Romal and had a very lively, insightful and fruitful discussion with her.

We have had known her from one of her session in our child's kinder garden school and were able to relate her advice, and thoughts over the period of time.

We again visited here (almost after 3 years) recently when we observed that we needed to work on our child's interest development in his studies or how to encourage him or work with him so that studies don't feel like burden to him.

We had very good discussion with her, her way of understanding things that parents facing, and explaining things and providing suggestion in very practical way shows her dedication in this era not only as a profession but as a service to society, especially to children who are suffering in studies and can't share their limitation, fear and sufferings.

Thanks again Romal ji.

- Ashish Bhawsar

I had the opportunity to interact with Romal when she helped carry out handwriting analysis for my daughters. The first thing that struck me when we went to meet, Romal was the serene positivity of her home-plus-office, which reflected in her interaction as well.

Romal's analysis was very accurate, and she could describe the characteristics of both my daughters to a great level of detail. She also sounded completely confident of her analysis, and explained to us how nuances within the handwriting of an individual reflect his/her personality. Romal went on to work on the areas where my daughters were facing challenges, and suggested methods to deal with them. I noticed that she was very straight and forthright with her feedback. My daughters have been practicing those methods and we have experienced a difference in those areas.

Overall, I would strongly recommend Romal as an experienced and skilled handwriting analyst.

- Abhijit Ray

It was as usual an awesome experience listening to the pearls of parenting. Realizing our own errors in the way. It was an eye opener. Especially the redeem points segment was a super cool methodology in Effective and efficient parenting. Romal Ma'am is par excellence and the vibes and energy she exudes puts the participants at ease and comfort. It reassures them of a mentor who is willing to walk the talk as well alongwith them as they mound their lil saplings to mighty oaks in the garden of humanity.

-Taapash Daszz